The Tea…
Personal … e
RE Cla…

Robert A Bowie
Director of the National Institute for Christian Education Research, Professor of Religion and Worldviews Education

Ann Pittaway
Research Fellow for Canterbury Christ Church University

GROVE BOOKS LIMITED
RIDLEY HALL RD CAMBRIDGE CB3 9HU

Contents

Anglican Association of Directors of Education

Acknowledgments

Grateful thanks to the Douglas Trust for funding the work behind this text and for the many other contributors who were involved at different stages of the process including: Dr Maria James, Nick Taunt and Emeritus Professor Trevor Cooling, as well as the many teachers and university tutors who respoded and fed back during early papers. Sincere thanks also to the Grove Education Series editorial team for their help in this final realisation.

First Impression January 2024
ISSN 2041-0964
ISBN 978 1 78827 365 7

1 Introduction

Who is This Book For, and Why Does the Teacher's Faith or Worldview Matter?

This book is intended for:

- Subject leaders of primary RE;
- Subject leaders of secondary RE;
- Christian ethos school leaders;
- Teachers responsible for SIAMS or Section 48 inspections;
- Teacher education tutors with responsibility for RE;
- School senior leaders responsible for staff induction, initial teacher education and staff development; and
- School governors.

The material is focused on the Religious Education (RE) classroom to help with the question of what you, as a teacher, choose to say about a personal faith or worldview you hold to when teaching. It is designed to help you consider how your own thinking, beliefs, and worldviews might affect the approach you take to teaching and ultimately shape the experience pupils have. We hope it will help you in the exercise of your professional judgment.

Teachers have different thoughts about whether they say or reveal anything about their personal faith or worldview, whether they are relaxed about participating fully in acts of collective worship in the school and whether they have visible indicators, through dress code or other worn symbol, of some connection to a specific religious or nonreligious worldview.

This book is first and foremost to help you as a teacher of RE or as a subject leader inducting new members of staff. It could also help any teacher who is concerned about the expression of personal views, beliefs or commitments in a professional context. Personal perspective can be conveyed in many ways—some explicit and others more subtle—so this book will explore how to manage expressing personal beliefs and worldviews within the classroom, while maintaining professional parameters and expectations.

Introductory Thoughts

As teachers we influence pupils and this is completely normal; it is, in fact, required in school if children are going to learn things from us. This influence operates at many different levels, conscious and unconscious. How one person is with another person makes some impact on them and many will remember the different kinds of interpersonal influence teachers have made on them. For teachers, navigating this influence is part of our professional responsibility.

How teachers hold the content or subject of the lesson is also an influence. Our interest in the material, our attentiveness to it and our beliefs about—and attitude to—it can be detectable. Whether a teacher is visibly bored by a topic or apparently fascinated by it can frame pupils' experience of the lesson.

Teachers have begun to discuss and explore the idea of worldviews in a big way, and this is usually in terms of the curriculum and what pupils are taught in class about religious and nonreligious worldviews. However, there is another angle to worldviews in the classroom. That is to do with what any worldview, belief commitment or philosophy of life that we have may mean for professional practice. While there are regulations and government guidance to advise on teachers' duties of political impartiality, alongside human rights responsibilities and promoting British values, religious and other non-political worldviews are a different matter.[1]

A Theological Concern

For a teacher operating within a Christian worldview (and this may mean within a culture we are not necessarily fully conscious of, or within a believing community we are conscious of) the question of influence and impact on others comes within a frame of ideas and practices associated with that worldview. There are several strands from which such a teacher might draw.

I might understand my role in terms of discipleship, as a learner myself, continuing to learn about God's creation through the ongoing field(s) that I and my pupils explore together in the classroom. In this formulation it is enough to be devoted to, and attentive to, the part of God's creation investigated by my subject since, as I discern more through my field, I see I move closer to God.

I might see myself as a more missional figure, in the world to be a Christlike example for others. While this accords with what many Christians see as a duty to bring others to Christ, much remains about *how* others may be brought to Christ, especially when working in a plural and diverse society and as a public professional, with public duties, responsibilities and codes of conduct.

It is helpful to distinguish between the leading role of the state school teacher, as a teacher of—and responsible adult among—pupils, and the spiritual disciple role associated with Christian mission. In some cases, teachers with well-meaning missional intentions might undermine that very mission, pushing away pupils and colleagues, perhaps to end up being censured.

The teacher is not the same as the missionary, the pastor or the priest, the healer, the carer, the protector or the defender, even if strands of these might come into play in teaching. This could happen when a teacher of a young child takes on the mantle of carer for a short while, or a senior teacher, in leading a collective act of worship, takes on features of the presiding role in a church service.

It might be helpful to see the (Christian) teacher as operating within a Christian worldview or Christian philosophy of education. This might be orientated by two other ideas:

> First, the *imago dei* doctrine, the idea expressed in Genesis that humans are made in the image and likeness of God. This is a human-centred idea that is itself a mystery, always held in balance with a human's sinful predisposition, yet pointing to an ultimate worth that is ordained in God's creative act of the person. This frames the teacher fundamentally as a figure of service to others, in response to their intrinsic dignity, rather than to any behaviour or achievement of the pupil. Intrinsic dignity relates to the status every human being has as a created child of God. In this understanding, to teach is to be servant to the pupil, whilst the teacher simultaneously holds an adult responsibility with associated duties determined by professional codes of conduct and requirements. For example, you attend to the age group specialist knowledge you need and subject area specialist knowledge which forms part of professional knowledge, this is then given in the service of the pupil, for a flourishing purpose which ultimately only God knows. In this way of thinking, humility is, therefore, a non-negotiable quality.
>
> Secondly, education is central to God's plan for the world, expressed in many ways in the Bible, not least in Genesis, through Adam's role of naming the creatures of the world as it unfolds. In a sense, Adam is established in that book as a learner and enquirer, a finder-out of things. Yet this too is held in balance with the danger that can come through learning, when it is separated from all other responsibilities and duties that humans have: to each other, to creation as a whole, to

morality and goodness. It is possible, in the pursuit of knowledge, to build a Tower of Babel of pride and selfishness, and the danger here is the act of hubris which can overwhelm curiosity, disciplined study and moral responsibility. Humans are intended to be learners, but not *only* learners, and not only learners *for themselves* in so far as they are social and moral creatures. The dedication to learning should include careful caution about the use of the power that comes with knowledge.

This brief introduction is enough to show that there is a balance to be struck between the different duties of the teacher, such as the philosophy of education of a church school. No individual Christian role or doctrine should be the sole influence on how a teacher achieves this balance. Rather, it is suggested that those working in education should understand that, whilst figures of authority in education, they also need to adopt a stance of humility and provisionality, being open to the impulse of the creative spirit or Holy Spirit. Teachers of many different beliefs and worldviews might find strong resonance with this idea.

What Is in It for the Teacher?

This book not only considers the professional context of the personal view, but it also seeks to encourage self-reflection, so as to develop a considered and informed approach to professional practice and integrity. It does not offer a final, total answer but hopes to encourage more confident and self-aware teachers navigating this question well.

Most sections begin with a brief introduction to an issue, then an illustrative vignette to earth the matter in real practice, followed by a set of reflective questions. Choose the questions that challenge. Some theory and research is also included to help you link your conclusions with the thinking of others. Thus the book can be used by individuals, but also by groups as a stimulus for discussion.

The Subject Debate and Personal Knowledge

2

What Is in a Name?

The teaching of religion in the UK's education systems has been subject to a few different names including 'Religious Instruction,' 'Religious Studies,' 'Religious Education,' 'Religious and Moral Education' and, more recently in Wales, 'Religion, Values and Ethics.' These names or titles alone have played a significant part in shaping others' perception of the subject. This is because each name or title bestowed upon it has been underpinned with the motive of framing and directing its purpose, content and delivery in the classroom environment. To consider three of these titles:

- *Religious Instruction*, the title used in the *Education Act 1944*, implied there was a 'how to' structure to being religious, or more specifically Christian, that required little self-reflection and inquiry but a significant amount of directive teaching from a proficient, practising instructor of the faith.
- *Religious Studies*, on the other hand, intended to shift the dissemination of the subject from the subjective study of religion to the objective. Such study was established in universities, where both teacher and pupil were encouraged to adopt an intellectual, impartial and comparative observance of the religious beliefs being considered. Essentially, under this guise the subject aimed to offer a detached, depersonalized lens through which religion(s) could be explored.
- The *Education Reform Act 1988* made the significant name change from *Religious Instruction* to *Religious Education* in schools. This paradigm shift established the subject as non-confessional and multi-faith in its approach. Under the influence of Michael Grimmitt, the subject developed two main aims that became commonly known as *Learning about* and *Learning from* Religion. While an academic objective approach to enquiring about world religions was essential, Grimmitt argued, 'We need to realize that religious concepts only come alive when we are able to relate them, sometimes partially, sometimes completely, to our own experiences.'[2]

There has been much debate about this connection between what is studied and the personal dimension.

Time for a New Vision?

In September 2018, The Commission on Religious Education, (CoRE) issued its final report, entitled *Religion and Worldviews: The Way Forward, A National Plan for RE.*[3] Alongside several suggestions, the final report recommended that Religious Education be renamed *Religion and Worldviews.* This was to establish two things. First, it was to set out the clear idea that everyone has a worldview (at least one!) and that the school subject should reflect that. Secondly it was to reflect the various religious and non-religious beliefs that contribute to our modern world. This report endorses the need to offer all pupils a broader and deeper encounter with the subject, whilst recognizing that, although some people perceive the world around them through a religious lens, others do not.

However, everyone inhabits a worldview, a lens through which our observation of the world is interpreted and lived.[4] It is recognized that modern society is composed of a complex labyrinth of worldviews that aligns with, nurtures, shapes and challenges our personal beliefs. Therefore it is imperative that young people are given the appropriate tools to develop a confident perception of their own beliefs and values, as well as an appreciative, empathetic understanding of others' differing views.

CoRE differentiated how the term 'worldview' can be understood. The term 'institutional worldview' describes organized worldviews shared among particular groups and sometimes embedded in institutions, incorporating both religious and non-religious perspectives. The term 'personal worldview' is applied to an individual's own way of understanding and living in the world, which may or may not draw from one, or many, institutional or shared worldviews.[5]

The Kinds of Knowledge Going On in RE

A fundamental concern of the CoRE report is the inconsistent quality of RE that pupils in this country are experiencing. The name shift of the subject, to include the term worldview, is aiming to make the subject more inclusive and relevant to all. The National Entitlement statements are designed to bring consistency and academic rigour to the subject.[6]

Richard Kueh, the RE subject lead for Ofsted at that time, presents the strands of knowledge that should inform quality RE.[7] He proposes the need for substantive knowledge (the content) and disciplinary knowledge (the ways of knowing emerging from sources of expertise), but he has also recognized the importance of the development of personal knowledge, encouraging pupils to explore their own worldviews.[8] While personal knowledge is not assessed according to whether it is the same as that of the teacher or the school's ethos, it is part of a pupil's perception of what is going on, and it is likely to influence discussion or debate and the expression of viewpoints.

Crucial to the successful development of pupils' personal knowledge is the teacher's awareness of his or her own worldview and the personal knowledge that they bring into the classroom. Whether teachers live a life committed to a particular worldview, or whether they are uncertain about any such commitments, or whether they are shaped by several, they do not stand apart from the currents of influence that flow into the classroom, including those that flow through them.

Ruth Flanagan's work on training primary school teachers in understanding their own personal worldviews found that an improved and expanding development of their *worldview consciousness* could not only improve their confidence as RE teachers, but could also lead to greater understanding of why others, with differing life experiences, might hold very different worldviews. Becoming worldview conscious equips teachers to move away from the superficial to focus instead on the underpinning values and beliefs expressed by different religion(s) and worldviews.[9]

Reflections

- What does the term *worldview* mean to you? What would it look like in a scheme of work, and / or a lesson?
- What challenges do you think schools face in terms of developing, or contributing towards, pupils' personal knowledge?
- Consider one aspect of belief, worldview or personal knowledge that is significant to you, such as parenting, teaching, marriage or gender transition, for example. What or who has influenced your approach to that belief or worldview? Where could there be tensions if you had to teach something about that topic in the classroom?

3 Expectations of the Subject Teacher

Teachers' Standards and the Faith/Worldview of the RE Teacher

The *Teachers' Standards* apply to all teachers in England, irrespective of what or who they teach or what stage they are at in their career progression: the *Standards* present a clear outline of the personal and professional conduct expected of teachers throughout their career. Part 2 of the *Teachers' Standards* relates to the personal and professional conduct expected of teachers as they maintain consistently high principles of practice. One of the key standards listed in this section states:

> Teachers uphold public trust in the profession and maintain high standards of ethics and behaviour, within and outside school, by:
>
> - ensuring that personal beliefs are not expressed in ways which exploit pupils' vulnerability or might lead them to break the law.[10]

This phrase might be linked to kinds of violent extremism and revolution; however, it could also be linked to ideological positions that attack or undermine the dignity of every human being, for example with racism. There is also a softer kind of influence that comes through the teacher-pupil relationship. Pupils are interested in what their teachers believe.

In a subject area where personal beliefs and worldviews explicitly contribute to classroom practice, the teacher of RE is in constant tension between upholding professional parameters and sharing personal views in a way that does not place undue influences on their pupils. Cooling suggests, 'The important question is this: is that influence undertaken responsibly?'[11]

Vignette 1

A teacher applying for a RE job in a church secondary school was given the following question to answer: 'What is the difference between Religious Education, nurture and evangelization?' This question was not only a tough one to answer, but it left a lasting impression on the teacher because she had never previously thought of the different ways her lessons could be framed and received within the classroom environment. Could her role as a professional be so clearly defined and compartmentalized? Was her primary role to nurture the faith development of the pupils in her care? Was she there to preach the gospel (evangelization)? Or was she there to encourage pupils to study religion in a purely academic way?

This happened at interview but more generally the place of personal beliefs or worldviews in the RE classroom is a contentious issue:

- Is there a boundary between disclosing personal insights on matters of faith and spirituality, and the professional practice of teaching?
- Can we, or should we, ever be expected to detach from our personal beliefs and worldviews when entering the professional public domain of the school and classroom?

These questions have been explored by Lynn Revell and Rosemary Walters in their work with student teachers.[12] They were aware that many believe non-religious people make the best RE teachers. The student teachers thought that passionate believers may seek to proselytize whereas someone who self-identifies as non-religious will be able to deal with religion and worldviews more equitably. Student teachers said things like:

- 'I think I would make a great RE teacher because, as someone who doesn't follow a religion, I am objective and I will be fairer.'
- 'My reservations lie in the worry that, as someone who follows a faith, it might be difficult not to let this sway my perception of things in the classroom, to be fair.'
- 'I do not want to seek to influence children in any way. That is not my work as a teacher of RE. I just need to tell them about religion.'

Revell and Walters interviewed student teachers from three universities and found that many Christian student teachers were concerned that overtly stating their beliefs would be unprofessional and prejudicial for pupils' learning, whereas most atheist or agnostic teachers believed that sharing their lack of belief or their own questions about the validity of faith could be a positive contribution to a RE lesson.[13] The two researchers discovered that the majority of the student teachers appeared to overestimate the influence of the teacher in the area of beliefs and values, to the extent that they believed they were able to change or influence pupils' beliefs merely by permitting pupil awareness of their own faith position.[14]

The former Archbishop of Canterbury, Rowan Williams, points out that people are not blank slates. Williams argues that in the actual historical world, people learn from a variety of stories, practices and relationships. And for the majority, these naturally and unselfconsciously include religious elements. The struggle to keep them out of view or to demand that they be dropped in a sanitized container at the entrance to any educational institution is not a sensible one in which to get involved.[15]

A detached teacher, who keeps secret his or her worldview identity, is also sending a message by not disclosing aspects of that identity, perhaps to keep personal views separate from a professional role or to try to keep focus on the pupils rather than the teacher. An agnostic teacher who promotes exploring and questioning might also become a promoter of not making a commitment, suggesting it is better to stay back from worldview and observe without committing. The situation is further complicated by the evidence provided by Erik Erikson, that young people are grappling with decisions about their identity early in their lives and these decisions are greatly influenced by their social environment.[16] Influence seems inevitable, so the teacher is left to determine what kind and how much.

Reflections

- Note any thoughts about, and responses to, Vignette 1.
- Is Rowan Williams right concerning the place of personal beliefs in education?
- Discuss an actual or hypothetical example of a teacher sharing what may be too much, or not enough, about a personal belief or worldview.
- Consider an example of when it might be easier to be non-religious *or* religious as a teacher of RE? And when might it be more difficult?

Becoming Aware of the Teacher that You Are

4

The Christian Positivist Approach and the Critical Realist Approach

Despite convictions within some education debates that teaching should be a neutral or objective process, Trevor Cooling's report, *Doing God in Education* argues that what you teach and how you teach it is heavily influenced by who you are and what you understand as being of value.[17] It is therefore important to recognize that, as a teacher, you do not teach in a value-free environment.

Everything taught and perceived, whether consciously or unconsciously, is filtered through language, culture and worldview, including any faith perspectives. For instance, different teachers may be issued with the same scheme of work and the same resources, yet how one person interprets and delivers these lessons will likely differ from the approach of another. People perceive things and present things with inflections they are conscious of and things they are unconscious of, which can include things they value. What a person values shapes what they see.

Speaking in the context of faith schools, Cooling argues that there are different ways of approaching an understanding of knowledge as Christians.[18] First, there is the *Christian positivist* approach, which holds the view that what a teacher knows about the Christian faith is true and so what is taught on it is true, thus the role as a teacher of Christianity is to persuade others to think likewise.

Vignette 2

A newly-appointed Head of Department for RE in a church school was given the task of finding out why pupils across the school were antagonistic towards RE. During week two of her appointment, she walked along the corridor to find that a pupil had been sent out of his RE class. On asking the pupil what was the cause of his dismissal, she was told, 'Miss, I got sent out because I said I didn't believe in God.'

The Head of Department spoke to the class teacher. The class teacher said the pupil was arguing for the non existence of God and so in sending him out of the class, she was upholding the truth of her faith and the ethos of the school.

This is an apologetic approach and, while apologetics as a discipline in its own right may be beneficial, in the context of a classroom Cooling argues it acts as a barrier. It shuts down alternative views with an emphasis on the assumed faith of the teacher being the measure of truth. It can leave a teacher feeling that their role in the classroom is to defend the faith to which they personally adhere.

So, is there an approach that can be taken which allows for different interpretations of truth to be voiced in a church school?

Cooling points to an alternative, known as a *critical realist* approach, which starts with the premise, 'I hold one truth, you hold another, so we need to work out why you understand a concept one way, while I understand it differently.'[19] Such an approach can bring personally-held views into an academic arena of disciplined discussion, dialogue and interpretation in the search of understanding, meaning and truth. There is an enquiry going on in the lesson, an exploration or learning journey of some kind.

In RE, the classroom offers a perspective on the ultimate enquiry, exploration and learning journey that humans engage in through religious and non-religious worldviews. It is also a subject that stretches beyond the limits of human knowledge, as notions of the holy or the divine, of ultimate value, of the possibility of a metaphysical or spiritual human purpose, all reach into territory that is a special territory to investigate. Bowie and Norman write (in the context of university education) about the value of 'a subject which pushes questioning to infinity, thereby allowing for insight, potential discovery and wonder.'[20]

Within such a subject, teachers can stay loyal to three responsibilities:

- to their own perspectives
- to the values of the school they work in
- to the values held by their pupils.

Each of these three responsibilities needs care and attention by the teacher, keeping it in balance with the others. There is a truth to be discovered, as well as an acceptance of epistemic humility—the acknowledgment that we are all fallible interpreters of truth, we have not finished finding out all the things that can be found out and there might be things about which we can never fully find out. In other words, a critical realist approach is anchored in the context of dialogue that recognizes truth is there to be uncovered, but it is important to recognize that we are susceptible exponents of such truth.

> We do not teach a value-free curriculum—if you do not have respect for diversity then you are in the wrong job. We have denominational education in some contexts / non-denominational in others, but they are all subject to professional standards with very clear moral and professional values. (RE lecturer)

Reflections

- Note any thoughts and / or responses to Vignette 2 and the above quotation.
- Consider the positivist and critical realist approaches to teaching described above. How might these insights influence classroom practice?
- Identify specific incidences or examples of when either the positivist or critical realist approach was applied in a classroom.
- Respond to the idea that we are all fallible interpreters of truth.

The Pupils in the Classroom

Each class that a teacher educates comprises a group of individuals whose minds are crammed full of ideas which frame their outlook and perspective on life.[21] Pupils can sometimes see themselves in the content of what is being studied, which in turn can raise questions about their own identity.

Vignette 3

An eight-year-old pupil went home after school and over tea said, 'Mummy, are we fundamentalist Christians or liberal Christians?' Mummy said, 'What do you think those words mean?' The girl said, 'Miss said that fundamentalists believe every word of the Bible is true, but liberals believe only that some of the Bible is true. You lead Sunday School at church and think the Bible is really important, so I suppose that means we are fundamentalists!' The girl's mother frowned and wondered if these terms were very helpful for explaining the faith life of their family.

How may I encourage a safe environment for the individuals within my classroom to feel confident in sharing their personal perspectives, without fear of rejection or ridicule from others? For some young people, peer pressure to think and act the same as the majority offers a safe sense of belonging, so opportunities to step beyond this security can mean that some in the class may remain silent or mask their true viewpoints. On the other hand, there may be individuals who are so intent on sharing their perspective that they completely disregard the views, or even the voice, of others.

Vignette 4

A teacher recalls teaching her first RE lesson in a faith school, when a pupil entered the classroom and declared quite loudly and boldly, 'I am an atheist and if you think for one minute you are going to brainwash me with all your Christian beliefs, think again. I'm not interested!' First, the teacher modelled an appropriate form of greeting someone and then said, 'I am interested to know why you hold an atheist belief?' The pupil replied, 'I don't know, but I just know I don't believe in God.' The teacher assured her that through RE, she would help the pupil explore her atheist views so she could give reason to them. The pupil was also assured by her teacher that she was not there to brainwash anyone. She became a very successful pupil, secure in her atheist outlook, and carried the subject on to A Level!

As teachers, it is important that we recognize we are role models of expected behaviour, whom pupils will observe, gain trust in and often emulate. Pupils and teachers also need to learn the art of dialogue, so that they have the appropriate tools with which to discuss and hear beliefs and views respectfully which both align with, and are different to, their own.

It is also important for the teacher to consider their questioning techniques. Are pupils encouraged, through carefully placed questions, to express and explore their views? Similarly, in responding with questions of their own, are pupils invited to delve further or are they simply shut down when their enquiry becomes too uncomfortable? Successful teaching has the relational at its heart and this is only developed through truly getting to know the class as a group of individuals with different strengths and needs. If individuals within the classroom are confident that others' views are received graciously and with interest, then they are more likely to offer their own.

Vignette 5

Following an A Level Religious Studies class on the creation narratives and interpretation, a pupil approached the teacher once her peers had left the room and said, 'I believe Genesis says that God created the world in seven days and I think that's literally true. I was embarrassed to put my view forward in class. A few of the pupils giggled when you explained the literalist view.' During the next lesson the teacher spent time looking at a literalist viewpoint in more depth so that the class gained a wider understanding of why this belief is upheld by some Christians. This gave that pupil the confidence to take ownership of her personal belief and speak about it, knowing that her peers, even though they did not have the same belief, were listening with understanding.

Reflections

- Note any thoughts and / or responses to Vignettes 3–5.
- What are some of the potential barriers that may prevent a pupil from sharing their personal perspective? How might these barriers be overcome?
- How can an environment of trust and openness be cultivated within the classroom?
- A pupil asks a question about belief that makes the teacher uncomfortable or lacking knowledge. How should the teacher respond?
- A teacher has a pupil who is being openly dismissive of another's belief. How might the teacher deal with this?

5 Freedoms and Limits

The School Context

Schools are micro-communities, built upon core values which direct their vision and influence their thinking. Moreover, schools usually have a vision or mission statement intended to steer the community through an educational environment, emphasizing exactly what is expected of all those concerned and outlining what it intends for the pupils in its care. Every individual operating within the framework of a school's vision has a responsibility to bring its formalized values to life through their daily practices and routines. As the writer, Gilbert Chesterton (cited in Haldane) states:[22]

> Every education teaches a philosophy; if not by dogma then by suggestion, by implication, by atmosphere. Every part of that education has a connection with every other part. If it does not all combine to convey some general view of life it is not education at all.

Contrary to common belief, even schools that claim to promote an environment driven by rationality, objectivity and neutrality are still holding true to an ideology. Gerald Grace states, 'There has not been, and in human society, cannot be a school or educational experience which is entirely autonomous, objective, neutral and ideologically free.'[23]

Thus, whatever school context a teacher works in, they will be professionally bound to carry out duties within the paradigm of its shared vision. Nevertheless, it is possible that, for practical reasons, a teacher finds they must operate in a climate of policies operating in the school, from government or religious authority, which are not ones they personally endorse. They may therefore find themselves in a position of some dissent.

To try to subvert the school leadership and values actively, prioritizing personal values which oppose those established by the school, establishes a significant conflict and undermines collective efforts in the school. It is wise, therefore, for any teacher working in a school to consider the vision and values that shape the school's environment. Spending most of your daily life in a school that has no resonance with your own values can be personally limiting and frustrating.

However, it may be that a school culture encourages a degree of dissent among teachers' voices and provides space for sensitively mediated discussion about values and policies which may be required and yet could seem controversial. Alternatively, it may be that in some cases, such as in matters of rights or school anti-racism policies, for instance, the legal duties are such that voices of dissent are not tolerated.

As part of the interview process for some jobs in many schools with Christian foundations, a teacher might be openly asked, *How will you support the Christian ethos of the school?* The response is significant because, whether a teacher's personal outlook is aligned to, or differs from, that of the school, they are exploring the teacher's understanding of the Christian ethos and how they would demonstrate the shared vision and values in their own practice. Although this does not form part of the interview process in community schools, be under no illusion, there is still an expectation that, as a member of their community, any teacher will endorse their shared principles.

Vignette 6

An English teacher, working in a Christian secondary school, was studying a piece of literature with his Year 9 class which focused on the issue of death and the afterlife. His lesson developed into a lively class discussion about heaven and hell. As part of the discussion, he offered his own beliefs, stating that he did not believe in life after death and that, when death occurs, that is the end as there is no heaven or hell. He left that lesson quite content with the pupils' engagement until the following morning, when a few phone calls from irate parents came through to his Head of Department, angry that their children came home from school saying, 'Mr X thinks death is the end and any belief in life after death is nonsense.'

Reflections

- How might someone be expected to react if they were expected to keep quiet about their beliefs on an issue?
- Does the balance between personal beliefs and the shared beliefs in a school community apply beyond the classroom? What about conversations with colleagues in the staffroom, or with parents at open evenings?
- What are the risks and advantages of being clear in the workplace about a person's religious or non-religious views?

- Why might some schools ask potential employees to endorse their ethos (religious or otherwise)?
- Is there a level of reasonable dissent? Are there some issues over which dissent should not be accepted?

Freedom of Faith/Worldview and Reasonable Expression of Identity in the Classroom

Before uttering a single word in a classroom environment, teachers may feel—and may be expected—to speak and work in such a manner that they:

- Invite all pupils to engage in disciplined learning and dialogue which respects their own and others' worldviews.
- Endorse the shared values of the school context in which the teacher practises.
- Stand in line with the *Teachers' Standards*, including the professional values (for example, individual liberty, respect, tolerance, the rule of law).

Hence, freedom to express personal beliefs in the classroom requires conscious awareness of your professional boundaries, as well as a great deal of personal discernment, humility and sensitivity. Some teachers take the view that sharing their personal stance can be obstructive and unnecessarily influence pupils' own thinking, while others believe that considered and appropriate disclosure of personal views can aid pupils' learning. How a teacher approaches this dilemma should be left to their professional judgment.

However, if there is an educational benefit to sharing personal beliefs, then it is essential to apply responsible and appropriate filtering to this practice. The main aim of any classroom environment is to create a safe intellectual and emotional space for every pupil; if personal opinion can contribute to this, as a tool for critical evaluation, then freedom to express what is believed may be heralded as an effective resource. If you are not sure what your beliefs will contribute or how you might influence, then it is probably best to remain silent. This is a route that some teachers choose, as much as to protect themselves as to protect the pupils. In life we do self-censor, especially when there is significant disagreement, controversy or conflict.

Freedom of expression within a classroom should always be anchored firmly within professional parameters. The Religious Education Council of England and Wales (REC) states:

> Teachers are influential people, and it is important that this influence is exercised in a professional and responsible manner, particularly in relation to religious and non-religious beliefs.[24]

Equally important is to understand that any personal expression of beliefs should be framed in such a way that they are not perceived as the final, absolute, agreed truth. It is easy for young people to think they can get clear-cut answers to all sorts of issues, when in fact such issues are invariably wrapped in complexity and layers of meaning. The REC document also states:

> Before sharing their response or belief with pupils, teachers…consider prefacing their thoughts with, 'My comments / beliefs are no more important than those of anyone else in this room / group' and are receptive to pupils' critical evaluations of their responses.[25]

In following this practice, the RE teacher is modelling the art of presenting a position in a respectful and non-threatening way, in the context of a world of plurality and diversity. Communities do develop confidence and faith around points of stability within themselves, but they also have mechanisms to live well in wider society, retaining space for dialogue and discernment.

Any expression of personal belief in the classroom not only needs to conform with the professional parameters already outlined but it also needs to be transparently articulated, without it being perceived as the correct and only belief. This is where the difference between Christian positivists and Christian critical realists shows. The former sees such strategies as compromise, the latter sees them as the exercise of intellectual virtue. This speaks directly to the philosophy of education a school has.

Vignette 7

These two scenarios exemplify the same issue within a primary school and a secondary school.

A primary student teacher, practising in a Church of England school with a Year 3 class, has just taught a lesson on the resurrection of Christ. He is accomplished and has used music, art and elements of drama in the lesson. At the end, one child raises his hand and asks if the student teacher believes that Jesus really came back to life again and if the story is true. The student teacher, a self-professed atheist, is being observed and wants to answer wisely but instead, blushes and says that he will speak to the child later. The child insists, 'But is it true?' The child is joined by others who sense the student teacher's awkwardness. The student teacher quietens the children and says RE is not about right or wrong answers. He is then saved by break time, but he knows this is not the last of the children's questions.

The Year 11 GCSE class is studying moral dilemmas around life and death, and today they have been looking at abortion and different views. About a third of the way through, a pupil asks the teacher what he believes about the subject. The teacher is a Christian who believes abortion is a grave sin, but he has a policy of never discussing his view in the lesson, and never before a given topic has been completed. He always says to pupils that the lesson is not about his belief but that at the end of the topic, after the lesson, the pupil can come and ask him what he thinks.

Reflections

- What responses might be given to the teachers' approaches in the Vignette 7 scenarios?
- What response might be given to the pupils' questions?
- What are the issues involved here: with young children, with older children?
- What might the pupils, in the given examples, assume by the teachers' responses?
- How might the kind of school a teacher is in have an impact on their attitude towards sharing personal beliefs?
- If a teacher holds a particular view on a contentious issue (such as abortion), what parameters might they set to filter themselves appropriately?

More than Just Words

6

Communicating Through Actions and Behaviour

Human beings articulate personal story through actions as well as words. As teachers we are role models for younger people, which includes being a figure of integrity—someone who is a professional but also someone who holds personal convictions and commitments. There is a link between personal behaviour or identity, and who I say I am. This is a matter of authenticity, of not being false. The danger of trying too hard to detach self from what we teach is that our spoken words remain lifeless, relegated to what Terence McLaughlin refers to as mere *edu-babble* (cited in McDonough).[26]

School communities may be established on a vision, or something called a mission (which may be corporate rather than necessarily religious), or a philosophy of education. These are transmitted through value statements, the way schools are organized, messages from senior leaders in the school and, perhaps most fundamentally, through the culture (or cultures) practised in the life of the school.

As a member of a school, we must decide how we negotiate with this corporate self-understanding. Are you an absolute loyalist or a collegial dissenter? Do you live a different identity at work from that of home, or are you a subverting revolutionary? Teachers may embody different roles accordingly, whilst schools may permit different degrees of corporate loyalty, collective responsibility and individuality among the staff body.

When teaching, my classroom becomes the platform for my pupils to learn from, or learn despite. My embodied example as a human, as well the subject and professional knowledge that I have, all come into play. Gaining the respect and trust of pupils, through the way we communicate a welcoming, safe and dignified space for them to flourish in, is essential. Haim Ginott's words act as a very apt reminder—that, as a teacher:

> I have come to the frightening conclusion that I am the decisive element. It is my personal approach that makes the weather. I possess tremendous power to make life miserable or joyous. I can be a tool of torture or an instrument of inspiration. I can humiliate or humour, hurt or heal. In all situations, it is my response that decides whether a crisis is escalated or

de-escalated, and a person is humanized or dehumanized. If we treat people as they are, we make them worse. If we treat people as they ought to be, we help them become what they are capable of becoming.[27]

Vignette 8

A pastoral lead in a secondary school was in a meeting with an irate parent whose child, she believed, was being unfairly picked on by her RE teacher. She told the pastoral lead, 'Ok, I accept that my daughter is not always the best behaved, and at the beginning of the year she rudely answered Mr X back in class, but we are now in the last term and ever since that incident, he always picks up on the slightest thing she does, while others in the class are getting away with it. What really angers me and my daughter is that he teaches about forgiveness and how important it is to forgive others when they hurt you, yet he obviously has not forgiven her. How hypocritical is that?'

It is worth balancing this strong statement with another truth. Teachers teach in a context, comprised of an institution that shapes them, the plural and diverse pupil population and the cultures and communities that they come from. The teacher may always be a decisive element, yet they are never the only element. Other factors may at times overwhelm a teacher's best intentions.

Reflections

- How might a teacher in that meeting with the parent react?
- Consider the different ways in which a teacher might articulate worldview/beliefs without words—in a classroom, in the school corridor and in the staffroom.
- It is much easier to express respectful, forgiving, hospitable values to those who reciprocate and appreciate your actions. Consider how a teacher would uphold such values in the following situations:
    - ◊ A pupil who consistently shows a begrudging attitude towards you.
    - ◊ A member of your department who is constantly undermining your work/resources.
    - ◊ A parent who complains about you, saying you are not doing enough for his/her child.

Communicating Through Dress Code

When teachers display their religious identity through wearing symbolic clothing and artefacts, head teachers, parents and pupils may make assumptions about those teachers' values and beliefs. For example, they may make assumptions about the nun who teaches RE or the Sikh teacher who wears a *Kara*.

There have been cases where teachers have been asked to remove symbolic articles of clothing as if the removal of outer trappings will temporarily suppress evidence of belief. Dianne Gereluk maintains there are several reasons why schools might ban symbolic clothing and artefacts.[28] These concern health and safety, matters of oppression and / or clothing significantly inhibiting the educational aims of the school.

Gereluk cites the French case of 2004 where all ostentatious religious symbols in school were banned. She points out that one reason for this ban was to create a stronger national identity and build a more cohesive and stable society. However, as she points out, the idea that a neutral space can be achieved by simply removing symbolic dress is unrealistic and naïve, believing that such legislation closes debate on how individuals can live in diverse and pluralistic societies.

Allowing both children and teachers to express their religious identities through what they wear encourages children to see and understand lifestyles other than their own, and this can be an effective strategy in building societal cohesion. However, there are practical challenges over how this is integrated into school policy and practice, as well as how much freedom a school gives to pupils who wish to express aspects of their identity visibly. Uniform policy can be challenging, especially when there are strong differences among the religious communities a school may serve: different countries reach different settlements about how they balance civic duties and religious rights.

Reflections

- What are the issues around these possible teacher practices:
  - ◊ To teach with an ash cross on the forehead on Ash Wednesday?
  - ◊ To wear a *Hijab*?
  - ◊ To wear a *Kirpan*?
  - ◊ To wear badges related to political movements?
  - ◊ To wear symbols linked to ethical movements?
- Imagine a teacher was asked to remove an article of religious dress by their head teacher. How might they react?

- In school dress codes, how would a teacher draw the line between individuality and freedom, alongside conformity to tradition or community? How might each of these have importance and present challenge?

Finally

Good teachers of RE need to express personal beliefs and worldviews with care and sensitivity in the classroom. Freedom to share personal beliefs within classroom practice is underpinned with a huge measure of professional responsibility and discernment. If shared without due care, such beliefs can, through words and actions, be detrimental to a positive classroom environment, the learning of pupils and even a teacher's own career. However, if negotiated through the correct professional boundaries, personal beliefs can have a valuable part to play in the classroom experience.

As a professional operating in a public domain, a teacher should use their beliefs only as a resource to advance and add depth to learning. Young people can learn much from a disciplined dialogue which allows for scrutiny and challenges to personal perspectives, within the safety of a classroom.

If a teacher is willing to place their own worldview or belief into this arena, while simultaneously respecting the views of others, pupils are likely to model this in the development of their own personal knowledge. Positive role models matter in life. Such exposure prepares young people for a modern world of diversity, allowing them to steer through conflict and challenge with a humbling confidence. It helps them grow in awareness that human understanding, both personal and collective, is multi-layered, complex and fluid, rather than compartmentalized and rigid. Personal knowledge and belief is a powerful tool for the classroom, so it is best used wisely.

Further Reading for Study

The following links may be of interest to you if you wish to consider further some of the ideas mentioned here:

J Arthur, D Moulin-Stożek, J Metcalfe and F Moller, *Religious Education Teachers and Character: Personal Beliefs and Professional Approaches, Research Report* (Birmingham: University of Birmingham, 2019).

T Cooling, *Doing God in Education* (London: Theos, 2010).

T Cooling with R Bowie and F Panjwani, *Worldviews in Religious Education* (London: Theos, 2020).

Religious Education Council of England and Wales, *Everyone Matters in the Classroom. A Practice Code for Teachers of RE* (London: Religious Education Council of England and Wales, 2009) (accessed summer 2023).

N Richardson, *Sharing Religious Education: A Brief Introduction to the Possibility of an Inclusive Approach to Religious Education in Northern Ireland* (Birmingham: Christian Education, 2014).

R Wormeli, *Do Teachers Remain Neutral or Share their Beliefs with Students?* (2016), https://www.amle.org/Portals/0/pdf/amle_magazine/sp/AMLEMag_Oct2016s.pdf (accessed summer 2023).

Notes

1 https://www.gov.uk/government/publications/political-impartiality-in-schools/political-impartiality-in-schools (accessed summer 2023).

2 M Grimmitt, *What Can I Do in RE? A consideration of the place of religion in the twentieth-century curriculum with suggestions for practical work in schools* (Great Wakering: Mayhew-McCrimmon, 1973) p 52.

3 Commission on Religious Education, *Religion and Worldviews: The Way Forward, A National Plan for RE* (London: Religious Education Council of England and Wales, 2018).

4 T Cooling with R Bowie and F Panjwani, *Worldviews in Religious Education* (London: Theos, 2020) p 46.

5 Commission on Religious Education, *Religion and Worldviews, op cit.*

6 *ibid.*

7 R Kueh, Religious Education Lead for Ofsted, REXchange online Conference 2020, 3 October 2020.

8 *ibid.*

9 R Flanagan, 'Teachers' personal worldviews and RE in England: a way forward?' *British Journal of Religious Education*, DOI:10.1080/01416200.2020.1826404 (2020).

10 Department for Education, *Teachers' Standards (London: Department for Education, 2011) p 14.*

11 T Cooling with R Bowie and F Panjwani, *Worldviews in Religious Education, op cit.*

12 L Revell and R Walters, 'Christian Student RE teachers, Objectivity and Professionalism: A research project based on interviews with student teachers from three universities investigating the way student RE teachers understand the relationship between their faith and professionalism' (Canterbury: CLIENT Faculty of Education, 2010).

13 *ibid,* p 4.

14 *ibid,* p 26.

15 R Williams, *Archbishop of Canterbury: Speech on Church Schools: A National Vision,* http://www.anglicannews.org/news/2006/03/archbishop-of-canterbury-speech-on-church-schools-a-national-vision.aspx (2006) (accessed summer 2023).

16 'Self-Identity in Children: Theory, Definition and Issues,' *Study.com*, 6 February 2017, <study.com/academy/lesson/self-identity-in-children-theory-definition-issues.html> (accessed summer 2023).

17 T Cooling, *Doing God in Education* (London: Theos, 2010).

18 T Cooling, 'The Return to Worldview: Reflections from the UK,' *International Journal of Christianity and Education,* 23(1), <https://doi.org/10.1177/2056997118818402> (2019), pp 3–9 (accessed summer 2023).

19 *ibid,* pp 3–9.

20 R Bowie with R Norman, 'Questions open to infinity and the legitimacy of wonder in university curricula,' *Journal of Religious Education* https://rdcu.be/czZtVhttps://doi.org/10.1007/s40839-021-00146-6 22 (published online October 2021) p 389 (accessed summer 2023).

21 P Steedman, 'On the Relations between Seeing, Interpreting and Knowing,' in F Steier (ed), *Research and Reflexivity* (London: Sage, 1991).

22 J Haldane, 'Chesterton's Philosophy of Education,' *Philosophy*, 65(251), *JSTOR*, www.jstor.org/stable/3751244 (1990) p 65 (accessed summer 2023).

23 G Grace, *Catholic Schools: Mission, Markets and Morality* (London: RoutledgeFalmer, 2002).

24 Religious Education Council of England and Wales, *Everyone Matters in the Classroom. A Practice Code for Teachers of RE* (London: Religious Education Council of England and Wales, 2009).

25 *ibid,* principle 5.

26 G P McDonough, *Beyond Obedience and Abandonment: Toward a Theory of Dissent in Catholic Education* (Montreal: McGill-Queen's University Press, 2013) p 118.

27 H G Ginott, *Teacher and Child: A Book for Parents and Teachers* (New York: The Macmillan Company, 1972) p 15.

28 D Gereluk, 'What not to wear: Dress codes and uniform policies in the common school,' *Journal of Philosophy of Education*, 41(4), https://doi.org/10.1111/j.1467-9752.2007.00576.x (2007) pp 643–657.